Exercises for Independence of the Fingers

By

I. PHILIPP

IN TWO PARTS

Formerly S.S.S. 49-50

Ed. 1545

G. SCHIRMER, Inc.

DISTRIBUTED BY

HAL•LEONARD®
CORPORATION

7777 W. BLUEMOUND RD. P.O. BOX 13819 MILWAUKEE, WI 53213

To I. J. Paderewski.

Exercises for Independence of the Fingers.

Example of Modulation.

I. PHILIPP.

All exercises are to be transposed, following the illustration given above. Practise slowly, with a very supple arm, and strong finger-action, depressing each key to the bottom with a full, round and even tone.

Only the two first harmonic forms of each exercise are given, the remaining ten transpositions having to be thought out by the player, who is by this means prevented from practising in that dull, mechanical way which so often acts disastrously on the musical instincts of even the most gifted. With this simple material, — and brains, — with patience, conscientiousness, and careful attention, one will infallibly acquire, in a short time, absolute independence of the fingers.

1st Series.

3

2nd Series.

Lento.

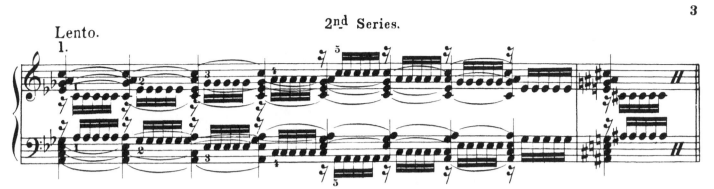

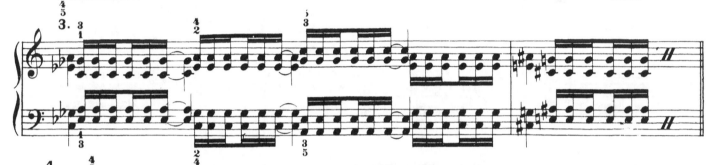

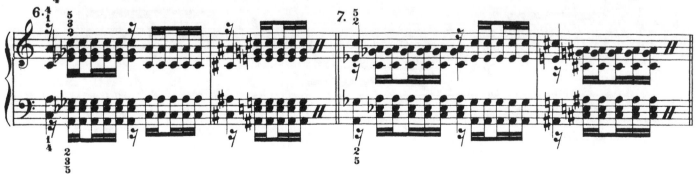

13784

4

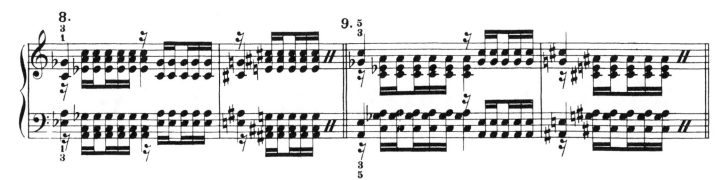

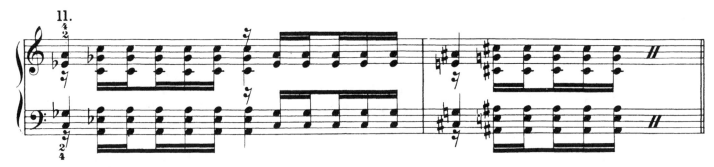

13784

3rd Series.

Lento.

1.

2.

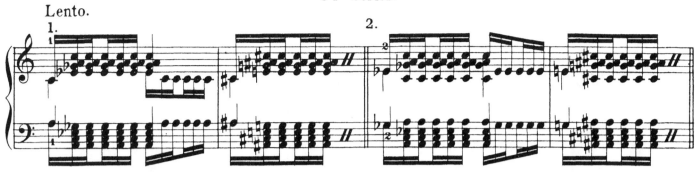

3.

4.

5.

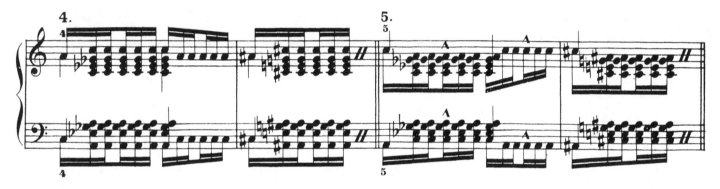

4th Series.

Lento.

1.

2.

3.

4.

5.

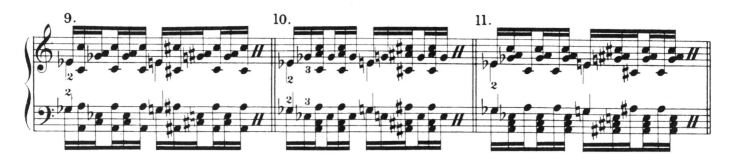

5th Series.

(Practise in parallel motion, and also in contrary motion.)

6th Series.

Allegretto.*)

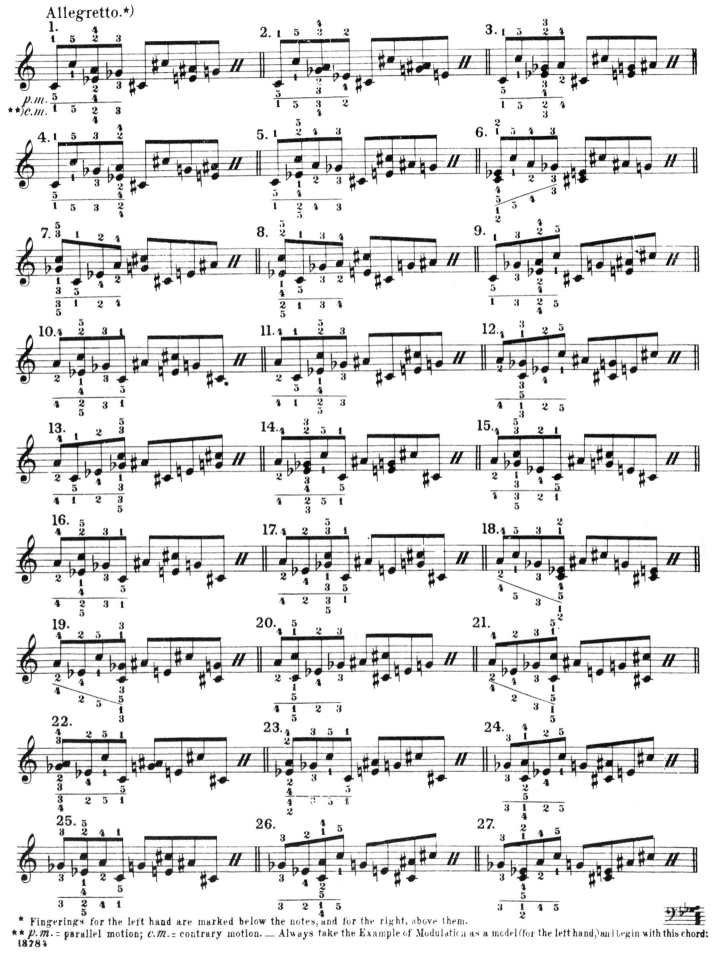

* Fingerings for the left hand are marked below the notes, and for the right, above them.

** *p.m.* = parallel motion; *c.m.* = contrary motion. — Always take the Example of Modulation as a model (for the left hand,) and begin with this chord:

18784

10

13784

7th Series.

(in contrary motion)

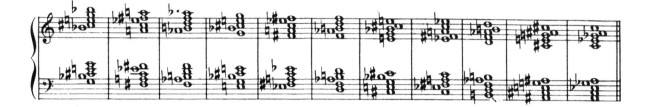

Vivo. (in contrary motion)   8th Series.

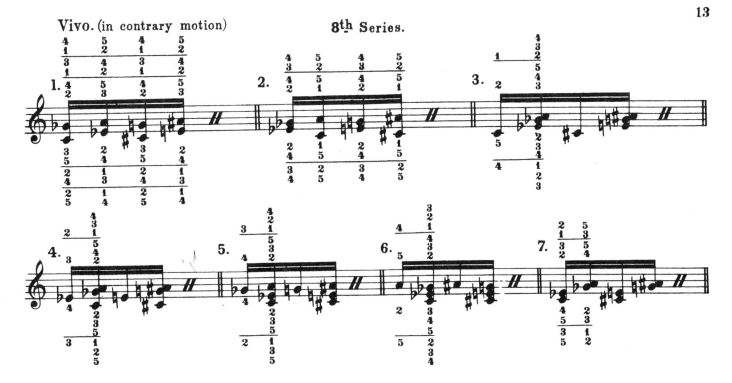

Vivacissimo.

Allegro. 9th Series.

10th Series.

Moderato.

Vivo.

11th Series.

13784

12th Series.

Presto.

1.

2.

3.   **4.**

5.   **6.**

Moderato.   (In contrary motion.)

7.   **8.**

9.   **10.**

11.   **12.**

13.   **14.**   **15.**

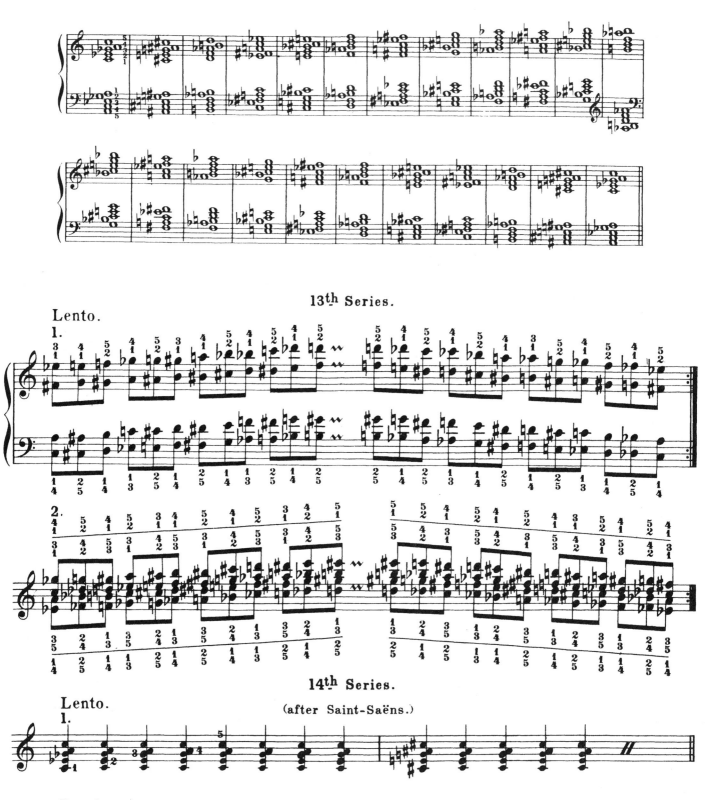

13th Series.

Lento.

1.

2.

14th Series.

Lento.

(after Saint-Saëns.)

1.

Presto.

2.

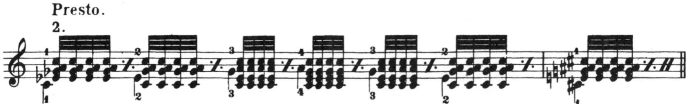

Vivo.

3. **4.** **5.** **6.**

(together.)

7. **8.** **9.** **10.**

Presto.

11.

12.

13.

14.

15.

Lento.

16. **17.**

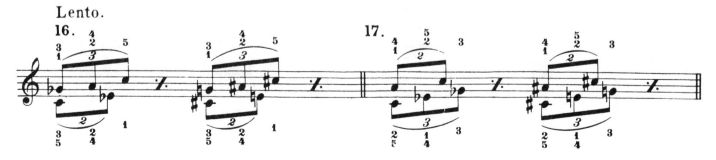

15th Series.

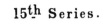

Vivacissimo.

16th Series.

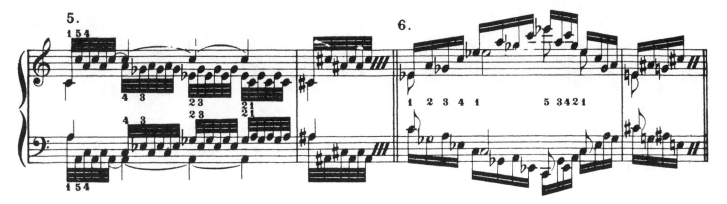

17th Series.

Leggierissimo.

Prestissimo.

13784

18th Series.

Series 6 and 7 may be practised with this same chord:

Examples (6th Series) (from 1-53):   (7th Series) (from 1-48).

Conclusion.

1. *Molto lento e pesante.*

staccato

2. *Molto lento e pesante.(from the wrist.)*

13784